To
MY MOTHER

CONTENTS

CONTENTS

INTRODUCTION

AS a country preacher in the lowlands of eastern Carolina I lived literally by still waters. Here is a serene retreat for him who cares to live a day at a time with leisure to "linger, list and dream": cypress swamps low-hung with moss; lazy waters where fishing-boats float carelessly; darkies abundant—another proof of leisureliness!—and everywhere the calm of restfulness that seems to drift in with the tide from the near-by sea.

For one who easily grows tired of modernity's mad masquerade it is pleasant to return to these tranquil lowlands. Nothing is more restful than a stroll beside these still waters while the wood-thrush serenades from the cypresses, while cattle amble homeward along pasture-lanes, and darkies hum their way from the fields at sundown.

Is it not significant that most of the men of God in the Bible knew best the fields, the pastures, the woods and waterways? Abel, the keeper of sheep; Abraham, Joseph, Moses, learning their deepest lessons among the flocks; David, the ideal shep-herd-boy, whose later psalms breathe so often the spirit of early days among the quiet hills; Amos, the herdsmen, John the Baptist, the fishermen-disciples, and, above all, the Lord Jesus—these knew the way of the still waters.

But drowsy waters alone cannot rest the soul. Yet these pleasant waterways of earth have their counterpart in the Word: *"He leadeth me beside the still waters."* In the terrific pace of this age men break in body, mind and spirit, and he who knows not God's waters of quietness knows no peace at any price. By Stoic hardihood, by "drowning their troubles," by forced optimism, by psychologic fads and freakish mental calisthenics, men seek

> *"That blessed mood*
> *In which the burden of the mystery,*
> *In which the heavy and the weary weight*
> *Of all this unintelligible world*
> *Is lightened."*

But they find it not. Partly, because it is not a mood, "a feeling fond and fugitive." It is a matter of faith, taking God at His Word. We reach the still waters when we cease being Ponce de Leons, looking for an elusive fountain of youth, and humbly follow the Good Shepherd to the green pastures. Men call that foolish, crude, childish,—there are so many newer, more up-to-date recipes for peacefulness. Everywhere fine boulevards lead to the popular resorts of this "ism" and that, where with clever new methods earth's doctors seek to treat the soul. But how often scholars ransack libraries looking for the secret of peace while the janitor may have found it long ago by the way of the Cross!

Do you know the waters of His rest? We do not mean that daily you will bask in happy circumstances. *"In the world ye shall have tribulation."* Our Lord's life was full of storm and tempest, yet in the darkest days of all He bequeathed to us His legacy of peace (John 16:33). His rest is no imaginary escape from reality. His peace is that blessed consciousness that in the midst of trouble our real lives are beyond the reach of circumstance hid with Christ in God.

Blessed experience, possible for the humblest believer here and now! And blessed prospect still ahead for us when this mortal shall have put on immortality: *"A pure river of water of life, clear as crystal, proceeding out of the throne of God and of the Lamb!"*

I

STAY AT THE ALTAR!

IF your prayer through the years has been un-
answered, if your castles have tumbled and
fond dreams have failed and now it seems impossible for God to do mighty works in your life,
go back and read the first chapter of Luke. It is
never too late with you this side of death for God
to work His wonders.

Zacharias and Elisabeth were remarkably quali-
fied for a life of blessing. They had good ancestry,
and that has its place even though the wag says
ancestry is like potatoes—the best part is always
under the ground! They were "righteous before
God," not merely before men. They walked in
all the commandments and ordinances of the Lord
blameless, not faultless but living up to their light.

With all that in their favour we might expect
every fortune to smile upon them. But "they had
no child." Have you sought to do His will through
the years and to walk in His commandments
blameless, yet your poor life is barren: you can
point to no definite, visible results, no fruit for all
your faithfulness? You know in your heart that

your desire has been to be righteous before God, yet "there is no child," your piety has borne no progeny.

Zacharias had been praying all his life for a child and now, from the natural point of view, it was too late, but he never forsook his altar. His task may have grown tiresome and his heart heavy with the disappointment of lean, unfruitful years, but he kept offering incense, the symbol of thankfulness, when he had, it seemed, so little to be thankful for. Never desert your altar, drooping heart, though Heaven seems brass to your cry; never forsake your incense, and the angel will yet appear!

Now comes the herald from Heaven announcing to Zacharias that his prayer is heard, he shall have a son! God often waits until by every natural reasoning it is too late for the blessing, waits until with men it is impossible, then when we are broken and undone the angel comes! It is all so astounding that poor, human Zacharias doubts after all his years of praying. Because he doubts he is stricken with dumbness, for doubt always leads to dumbness. When we do not trust the Lord we have no testimony. But though Zacharias fails, God does not: the baby is born, and when neighbours would honour his father by naming the son for him, Zacharias puts God first and names him by the divine direction. Never dare to name things after yourself, give God the glory! And when God's will is done, dumbness gives way to delight; Zacharias speaks, and so will you! Putting God first will always loosen your tongue and give you a message!

If in your life "there is no child," no spiritual fruitage after all the years of faith, if you have prayed until it seems too late, I beg you, stay at the altar! As a boy I used to hear a saintly old mother rise in the little country church back home and ask for prayers for the conversion of her sons. I thought it was useless, so worldly and indifferent they seemed. Today, she has passed on, but three of those sturdy boys are faithful Christians in that same little church, and one is a deacon and leader. That mother knew what I had not learned, to stay by God's altar.

If most of life has gone and what is left looks bleak and desolate, if by very earthly reason it is too late for your prayers to come true, do not give up your place before the Lord. God never forgets His appointments. The angel will come!

II

BIBLE WINDOW-SHOPPING

A FAMILIAR figure on the streets is the window-shopper who moves along gazing fondly in each show-window but buying nothing. In the realm of things spiritual we have with us the Bible window-shopper. He moves along through the Book reading its precious promises, hearing its high challenges, looking at its deep messages of peace and power and victory. But he never makes them his own. He appreciates but does not appropriate. He respects his Bible, argues for it, counts it dear, but its rich treasures never become living realities in his own experience. He is a window-shopper amongst the storehouses of God's revealed truth.

On the way, he passes by where is displayed such a choice jewel as *"We know that all things work together for good to them that love God, to them who are the called according to His purpose."* "What a rare pearl that is!" he exclaims. "What a lofty faith one needs to believe that!" So he moves on and the treasure stays on exhibition. He does not go in and claim it, though, if he be a believer, it is his and is there for him. He is only window-shopping.

How many believers loiter along the Bible stores' and come away empty. *"My God shall supply all your need according to His riches in glory by Christ Jesus."* One reads that devoutly and, an hour later, is worrying about adversity and bemoaning his hard circumstances! *"They which receive abundance of grace and of the gift of righteousness shall reign in life by One, Jesus Christ."* Another looks at that gem and lives like a pauper when God meant him to be a prince. *"All things are yours";* there are many who behold that free pass to all God's unlimited stock, yet live spiritually almost bankrupt. Window-shoppers!

The storehouse of God's Word was never meant for mere scrutiny, not even primarily for study, but for sustenance. It is not simply a collection of fine proverbs and noble teachings for men to admire and quote as they might Shakespeare. It is rations for the soul, resources of and for the spirit, treasure for the inner man. Its goods exhibited upon every page are ours, and we have no business merely moving respectfully amongst them and coming away none the richer.

The window-shopper upon the streets often has a very good reason for not buying: he has not the wherewithal. But no believer can say that of God's riches, for the treasure of His Word is without money and without price. Whosoever will may drink freely. Some window-shop because they never have fully realized that the things of the Spirit can be made actual, living realities here and now amidst this humdrum, daily round of commonplace duties. Others loaf along, indifferent to their inward poverty, faring scantily when the banquets of God are at their disposals. And some substitute wishful longing for the practical realization of the Christ-life.

The Lord is rich unto all who call upon Him. Let us have done with this idle window-shopping. Let us go into the deep stores of His Word, rummage among its treasures new and old, and come forth from each excursion laden with the bounty in the Book.

III

THE DESIRES OF THINE HEART

LIFE, for the Christian, does not always run along in story-book style. The hero is not always crowned, the honest do not always get rich, nor does the noble knight invariably claim the princess and live happily ever after; sometimes it happens, but oftener it does not.

This leads weak believers to question God's promises and live in the doldrums because their faith is not the password to every garden of desire. They fail in business, they get sick, they lose their dearest ones, they plug along at some mediocre job, and then because their trust in God did not pull down the plums they charge the Almighty with sending them crab-apples.

I know how such people feel, for I, too, have been familiar with tumbled castles and fading dreams. I used to read (Psalm 37:4): *"Delight thyself also in the Lord: and He shall give thee the desires of thine heart"*; and I wondered how it could be true. It did not seem to work in my case. Most of the things I'd craved seemed to have gone to somebody else. I stood in the harbour and watched others unload the cargoes of dreams come true, but my ships did not come in.

Today I believe more than ever in the promises of God. For one thing, God has promised us that we shall have trouble in this world. *"In the world ye shall have tribulation"* (John 16:33). *"All that will live godly in Christ Jesus shall suffer persecution"* (2 Tim. 3:12). These are promises just as surely as are the assurances of good things. We must take all the promises into our calculations. God has not guaranteed to save me from the adversities common to man, but He has written that He will keep me in the midst of them. So, when I have trouble, that is one promise being kept, and when He sustains me in trouble, He is keeping another promise. Remember that when Jesus said we should have tribulation in the world He added, *"but be of good cheer; I have overcome the world."*

What about the desires of mine heart? If I delight myself in the Lord and want a million dollars, shall I get it? Faith in God is not an easy path to *self*-satisfaction. What is the true desire of one whose delight is in the Lord? *"Not my will, but Thine."* When we are living in Him our wish is that His will be done. And when this is the desire of our hearts, He will give us our desires.

Faith in God will not get for you everything you may want, but it will get for you what God wants you to have. The unbeliever does not need what he wants: the Christian should want only what he needs. And God has promised to supply our need according to His riches in glory by Christ Jesus. That is enough, for what we do not need can do us no good.

The believer should pray, "I want this thing, if it be in Thy will." If he does not get it, then it will be because it was not in God's will; and if it was not in His will, then he did not spiritually desire it. In this blessed state that delights in the Lord there can be no disappointment.

If you are doubting Psalms 37:4, the trouble is not that the promise has failed. You simply are not keeping the first half of the verse, the condition of the promise. If you really delight in Him, your desires will be the kind He has promised to satisfy.

IV

GOD'S CURE FOR FAINTING

FAINTING is a common experience in our spiritual lives. The Word has much to say about it and provides a remedy for it.

The wise man said, *"If thou faint in the day of adversity, thy strength is small"* (Prov. 24:10), but most of us do. Like Job, we comfort others in trouble, but when it comes upon us, we faint (Job 4:5). Like Jeremiah we must say, *"When I would comfort myself against sorrow, my heart is faint in me"* (Jer. 8:18).

God does not want us to be faint-hearted. Directing Israel as to their conduct in war, He advised through the priest, *"Let not your hearts faint"* (Deut. 20:3), for He knew such a soldier could not fight. There is another reason: in the same chapter the officers were bidden to say before the battle, *"What man is there that is fearful and faint-hearted? Let him go and return unto his house, lest his brethren's heart faint as well as his heart."* The ideal soldier is like Gideon and his three hundred who, in Judges 8:4, *"came to Jordan and passed over, faint, yet pursuing them."*

[19]

"Faint, yet pursuing!" What sermons in that! The church at Ephesus was commended because it had laboured and had not fainted (Rev. 2:3).

The Lord Jesus Christ would have us *"pray and faint not"* (Luke 18:1). We have a Gospel to proclaim, and must not faint (2 Cor. 4:1). We should not faint at the hardships of Christians (Eph. 3:13), but *"consider Him that endured such contradiction of sinners against Himself, lest ye be wearied and faint in your minds"* (Heb. 12:3). We are not to despise God's chastening nor faint when rebuked of Him (Heb. 12:5). And *"let us not be weary in well doing: for in due season we shall reap (a reward) if we faint not"* (Gal. 6:9).

The Lord Jesus Christ is compassionate on us when we are faint (Matt. 9:36). What are we to do when we faint? Like Jonah: *"When my soul fainted within me I remembered the Lord"* (Jonah 2:7). Like the Israelites: *"Hungry and thirsty, their soul fainted in them. Then they cried unto the Lord in their trouble, and He delivered them out of their distresses"* (Psa. 107:5, 6). Like the Psalmist: *"My soul fainteth for Thy salvation: but I hope in Thy Word"* (Psa. 119:81).

But the richest passage for the faint is Isaiah 40:28-31. There is something about fainting in every verse. Let us look first at verse 28: *"Hast thou not known? hast thou not heard, that the everlasting God, the Lord, the Creator of the ends of the earth, fainteth not, neither is weary?"* God does not faint. How precious to know there is One Who wearies not! One Who, as the everlasting Creator, upholds all His own in His everlasting strength.

Now verse 29: *"He giveth power to the faint."* That is what we want; there is our Resource. Verse 30: *"Even the youths shall faint."* Alas, that has been our sad experience: there is our plight. But victory awaits in verse 31: *"They that wait upon the Lord . . . shall walk and not faint!"* And our part is only to wait upon the Lord!

But we do not like to wait nowadays. We want to rush ahead and take matters in our own hands, and so we soon play out, we are out of breath, we faint. And nothing better could possibly happen to us, if it will bring us to the end of ourselves and to wait upon Him. It is either faith or failure: if we do not trust Him we shall assuredly collapse. How perfectly the Psalmist summed it all: *"I had fainted unless I had believed to see the goodness of the Lord in the land of the living. Wait on the Lord: be of good courage, and He shall strengthen thine heart: wait, I say, on the Lord"* (Psa. 27:13, 14).

V

"ALL THESE THINGS ARE AGAINST ME"

OFTEN I have thought of old Jacob's re-
mark when his sons returned from their
first trip to Egypt. Things were in a bad
way for him. Joseph was lost, dead most likely.
Now Simeon was kept in Egypt as a sort of secur-
ity. And, still worse, Benjamin, the dearest child
of all, had to be sent along on the next trip and the
possibilities were uncertain. It was a dismal strait
for the old man and he groaned: *"Joseph is not,
and Simeon is not, and ye will take Benjamin
away; all these things are against me"* (Gen.
42:36).

So he thought. But, could he have seen behind
the dark face of things, and watched the divine
hand shaping the course of things, he would have
talked differently. Far from being against him,
the miserable developments he mourned were
working things out exactly in his favour. Joseph
was alive in Egypt, and the hand that seemed
hard was to become infinitely precious. Simeon
would be released, Benjamin would not be harmed,
there would be a blessed family reunion and all

live happily thereafter. Yet, poor, short-sighted Jacob lamented, *"All these things are against me."*

Is it not so with you and me? When things come to a wretched pass, and our fortunes sink to lowest ebb, looking at things as they appear with our poor vision, we think all things are against us. We measure the whole thread of life by a few black inches. We think that because things look dismal from our point of view they must be dismal from every point of view, God's included. Every plan goes awry, every arrangement works out wrong; the universe seems to have a grudge at us and Heaven seems solid and unresponsive to our cry. So we hang our harp upon the willows and grow disconsolate: *"All these things are against us."*

But just when everything seems to have gone into a coalition against us and, look where we will, no one can show us any good, then often God is working out for us His blessing. There is another verse which starts off much like Jacob's complaint, but how differently it ends: *"All things work together for good to them that love God, to them who are the called according to His purpose"* (Rom. 8:28). Now, a believer cannot believe both these verses. He must choose one or the other. If the latter verse be true, then the first cannot be. Jacob

[23]

was wrong. And so are we, when we talk as he did.

The course of things does not work against the believer. It may seem to. It may work against his earthly fortune. It may even appear to defeat him. But in the eyes of God and in the light of eternity all things work together for good. The world laughs at such doctrine as childish and rails on at Fate. Well, all things do not work together for good to everybody. The unbeliever has no part in it. Only to them who love God and are His does it apply. And the world cannot appreciate such simple trust in Him until it first has learned truly to love Him. Of course, it laughs and is sceptical and calls it blissful ignorance.

And so many of us who believe still doubt. We appreciate our verse, but we do not appropriate it. Jesus might have said in Gethsemane or at Calvary, *"All these things are against Me,"* but in the resurrection He proved that all things work together for good to Christ and to the Christlike.

It is either Jacob's attitude or that of the Lord Jesus. Where do you stand?

VI

"ACCORDING TO YOUR FAITH"

MY heart goes out to the believer who is earnestly seeking a fuller and deeper Christian experience. But the quest for the abundant life has become a sort of glorified hobby with all too many. They are ever learning and never able to come to the knowledge of this truth. They sing songs of the higher life and bemoan their weak and faltering existence. They run from preacher to preacher, hoping the next one will clear up the mystery. They devour devotional books—"surely on the next page I shall find the 'open sesame' to the life I crave!"

The Lord gave us the key long ago: *According to your faith be it unto you.* There is no use in looking for vague sensations and mystic raptures: here is the measure of the life triumphant. As you believe in Him, in proportion as you trust Him, so shall your experience be.

He did not say, "According to your fate." Some of this talk about "what is to be will be" is fatalism passing for predestination. If you are too lazy to launch out expecting great things from God and attempting great things for God, then do not blame your shallow life on divine Providence.

He did not say, "According to your fortune."
We buttress ourselves around with lands and
goods and think that means life abounding, but
*"a man's life consisteth not in the abundance of
the things which he possesseth"* (Luke 12:15).
The things may be abundant, but still the life
is not.

He did not say, "According to your fame." *"He
that ruleth his spirit is better than he that taketh
a city"* (Prov. 16:32). Taking cities—doing the
spectacular, getting in the headlines—may be exciting business, but it is not the ideal life. True
success is always in the realm of spirit: it may be
obscure and tucked away in some drab place
among unromantic people, but the really faithful
are the really famous.

He did not say, "According to your friends."
Popularity and "pull" are not the measure of fine
living. Friends are only human, frail and often
futile. And sometimes *"mine own familiar friend,
in whom I trusted, which did eat of my bread,
hath lifted up his heel against me."* It is well if
we can follow the Psalmist into the next verse,
"But Thou, O Lord!" (Psa. 41:9, 10).

He did not say, "According to your feelings."
There is our pet false measure: we think there
must be a "grand and glorious feeling" all the
time.

[26]

"Think not the faith by which the just shall live
 Is a dead creed, a map correct of Heaven;
Far less a feeling, fond and fugitive,
 A thoughtless gift, withdrawn as soon as given.
It is an affirmation and an act
Which bids eternal truth be present fact."

It is *"According to your faith."* It is for you
to set the bounds of your experience. If you trust
Him much, you shall realize much. The resources
are there: if you make small drafts on the bank of
Heaven, do not wonder if you are always ragged
and down-at-the-heel, rattling a few pennies, while
others are rich with God's gold. The Lord is rich
unto all that call upon Him (Rom. 10:12): you may
be rich, *"for all things are yours"* (1 Cor. 3:21).

Remember that faith is not a strange sensation
that comes over you in rare moments, a magic
thrill from something in the minister's voice, a
mystic trance to be reached once in a while, then
lost for weeks or years. It is a sturdy confidence
that God will keep His promises, confidence enough
to walk out on them and live there, although the
world expects them to crack and crumble under
you any day.

Don't waste your time looking for fancy recipes
in poems and books and lectures about triumphant living. You will triumph only as you trust:
as you have faith, so will you fare.

VII

FAITH IN PRAYER, OR PRAYER IN FAITH?

MANY have prayed earnestly for some definite blessing and then, when it failed to come, have grown bitter and even cynical. And one hears from such disappointed hearts the frequent refrain, "I have lost faith in prayer."

The very phrasing of that statement reveals a misunderstanding of the right attitude toward prayer. Faith in prayer is one thing; prayer in faith is another.

The man who starts out only with faith in prayer puts too much emphasis upon prayer and not enough upon the God to Whom he prays. He uses prayer as a sort of magic talisman, an "open sesame" to the things he wants, a quick way of getting things he wants from God. Then, when he does not get what he asks for, he gives up prayer much as the heathen beats his fetish when he gets into trouble. Prayer is really his god. Instead of being pious, he is, in a sense, idolatrous. Faith in prayer may be a very childish and inadequate attitude.

The object of our faith should be God rather than prayer. Then, prayer in such faith will not fail. We ought first utterly to commit all we are and have into His hands and leave them in His keeping. We ought to realize that while we can see only a tiny segment of life at a time, God sees the length and breadth of it with all its complications and intricacies. That being true, what we think we want may not, in His sight, be our need at all. So, when we pray in faith, faith in God, we first recognize that all things are in His hands and that He has promised to supply our needs.

So praying, we are prepared for our particular request being denied. God may say, "Wait" or "No." But, while He may deny the particular petition He never denies us. In that confidence we will not childishly sulk when this or that definite request is refused. For our faith is in God and, whatever may happen to a prayer, He is faithful.

Why pray at all if God meets our needs? So does a true parent meet the needs of his child; yet there are many things a child receives that it never would receive, if it did not ask for them. Not only that, but if a child is to receive its needs it must stay in communion with the parent. Prayer is not merely begging things of God; it is also maintaining communion with Him. It takes the gracious giver and the willing receiver to make a perfect gift. And prayer is the human soul opening its hand to the Giver. The child that trusts and loves its father is the one that is continually making requests. The more one trusts and loves the Father, the more he presents to Him the desires of his heart. True believers are not those who indifferently ask, "Why pray?" They are continually sending their petitions to the Throne of Grace, but they trust God to sort out their prayers and leave results to His discretion.

Faith in prayer may be a cheap thing, bordering on superstition, like knocking on wood. But prayer in faith, faith in God, is a sturdy, rugged confidence that presents humbly, yet boldly, its claims and leaves the rest with God.

VIII

A BOTTLE IN THE SMOKE

THE eighty-third verse of the one hundred and nineteenth Psalm runs as follows: *"For I am become like a bottle in the smoke; yet do I not forget thy statutes."* The reader misses the point here unless he remembers that the bottle is a vessel made of skin which becomes shrivelled and wrinkled when exposed to heat and smoke. So the Psalmist declares himself furrowed and dried up by sorrow, yet not forgetful of the Word of God.

In the heat of time and trouble all of us become, eventually, bottles in the smoke. Childhood cannot keep its rose-petal freshness. Men cannot stay handsome nor women maintain the schoolgirl complexion. Against this old Bible truth beauty-parlours wage war in vain. We must become like bottles in the smoke.

That much is inevitable. But if that part of our verse must come true, we can see to it that the rest of it becomes true with it: *"yet do I not forget Thy statutes."* If we must reap the wrinkles, we can

[31]

also remember the Word! And if only the time and money and energy spent in trying to avoid looking like bottles in the smoke were used in the study of the Word we should have a happy world. For wrinkles do not matter when we have treasured His statutes. *"The hoary head is a crown of glory, if it be found in the way of righteousness."* "The beauty of old men is the grey head."

Blessed is the man who meets life's inevitables with spiritual resources. I think of my father. In his last years he was very much like a bottle in the smoke. Cares and troubles had bent and wrinkled him. Life's heat and smoke had dried him up. But he did not forget the statutes. Often I overheard him sitting alone in his little grocery store pleading the promises in a low-voiced prayer. Life had marked his face, but life could not mar his faith.

Not long ago I attended a little prayer-meeting in the home of an aged couple too feeble now to attend church. It was a precious service with neighbours gathered in and the broken old man and his wife in place of honour. Time had devastated them: broken speech, failing eyes, trembling hands and furrowed faces told a tale of many years. They made a pathetic picture, but it soon changed. We were singing those familiar old lines,

"Through many dangers, toils and snares,
I have already come;
'Tis grace hath brought me safe thus far,
And grace will lead me home."

Tears coursed down wrinkled faces and a smile of confidence displaced the gloom. Time had not devastated them! They had become like bottles in the smoke. but they had not forgotten the statutes!

That is why Jesus bids us lay up treasure in heaven beyond the reach of moth and rust and thief. These work havoc with everything else. We soon become like bottles in the smoke. But, if we have hid His Word in our hearts, in the midst of our sorrows we can remember His statutes.

IX

A VOICE FROM HEAVEN

IN the midst of one of His discourses Jesus prays, *"Father, glorify Thy name,"* and a voice from heaven answers, *"I have both glorified it, and will glorify it again."* Then follow three interpretations of the voice by those who heard it. Some said it thundered; others said that an angel spoke to Him; Jesus said that it was God's voice speaking concerning His approaching death.

These three interpretations cover the whole range of our attitude toward supernatural revelation. God has been speaking to men through the ages. Some have heard nothing but thunder and have explained it all away by natural causation. Some have heard the angel: they do believe that there is intelligence and possibly personality back of the universe, and believe that our better impressions are something more than sensations stirred up by a frolic of atoms. There have always been a few who have gone further and believed with Jesus that God really has spoken in a revelation that transcends all ordinary inspiration.

[34]

These view-points hold true from any angle of God's manifestations of Himself. God speaks to us through nature. *"The heavens declare the glory of God and the firmament sheweth his handywork."* Some see only the workings of natural law; the Grand Canyon is but a cosmic accident; sunsets are purely physical, and nothing more. They hear only thunder! Others find earth crammed with heaven and every common bush afire with God. But the Christian goes even further and sees nature in the light of Christ, torn and groaning and travailing now, but one day to be restored to peace and harmony.

God speaks through the Bible. Some hear only thunder, it is only a book. Others believe it inspired as Shakespeare is inspired, but not a supernatural revelation—just the voice of an angel, not God. Others take Jesus' point of view. To them, the Bible does not merely contain God's Word, it is God's Word. His Word they hide in their hearts that they might not sin against Him.

But in the supreme revelation of all, *"God, who at sundry times and in divers manners spake in time past unto the fathers by the prophets, hath in these last days spoken unto us by His Son."* Some hear only thunder in the Christ, He was but a man now encrusted in legend and tradition. Others think He was inspired, perhaps the greatest of

[35]

men, but still a man. They hear the angel. But others hear more than man, they fill out "man" until it becomes "Immanuel"—God with us.

In the particular incident of John 12:28-32, God not only speaks through Christ, but to Him. Jesus goes on to explain that the voice spoke for the hearer's sake, and then speaks of His death in which the world is judged, Satan cast out and all men drawn to Him through His death. Jesus regarded His death as the centre and heart of God's purpose for Him. Naturalism, hearing only thunder, places no value on Christ's death. Modernism, hearing only the angel, regards Christ's life and teaching as more important. Both reject Jesus' own interpretation of God's testimony to Him. We have not caught the true and full meaning of God's revelation in Christ until we see that Calvary is the heart of it. Jesus is more than God speaking to men. He is God becoming man in the person of Christ to bear our sins upon the Cross.

Modern Greeks ask to see Jesus as did these referred to in John 12. But for all there is one answer: "It is not as teacher or ideal character that I am truly to be known. The corn of wheat must die. It is as the crucified and risen Saviour that you must know Me if you are to be saved."

God is speaking. Which way do you hear Him, as thunder, as an angel, or as Himself?

X

THE SHRUNKEN SINEW

THE crisis of Jacob's life came at Jabbok. He had done his best organizing to meet Esau. The time had come for agonizing. Unable to sleep, he was left alone, as all of us are in crises, and he wrestled with a heavenly visitor until break of day. We know the story, how he held on until he got the blessing. I am concerned with the other side of it: the mysterious wrestler put Jacob's thigh out of joint and we read that as Jacob passed over Penuel the sun rose upon him and he halted upon his thigh.

It was a glorious experience for Jacob. *"I have seen God face to face, and my life is preserved,"* he declared. He fared forth in fresh confidence to meet Esau. But he went with a shrunken sinew.

It has been so through the ages. Men who prevail with God bear the marks in shrunken sinews. Men who meet real crises, who come to the end of themselves and to utter trust in God have to be put out of joint somewhere. Jacob came forth from this encounter bearing the name Israel—"A Prince of God." God's princes are not the haughty, self-sufficient sort paraded now among

foolish advocates of "survival of the fittest." They
limp and are halt, for they have been put out of
joint that God might prevail.

We are reminded of the Lord Jesus' thrice-
repeated solemn statement: *"It is better for thee
to enter into life maimed than having two hands*
[or, feet or eyes] *to go into hell . . . where their
worm dieth not, and the fire is not quenched"*
(Mark 9:42-48). We think of Paul's thorn in the
flesh, the messenger of Satan to buffet him, lest he
should be exalted above measure. God's princes
often must bear the shrunken sinew of some
humiliating mark or memory to remind them of
their own frailty and that God's grace is sufficient,
His strength made perfect in their weakness.

Why was Jacob's thigh put out of joint? In
order that God might prevail, and then in order
that Jacob might prevail to receive the blessing.
If Jacob had prevailed in wrestling, his victory
would have been in his own strength, and he
would have been harmed instead of helped. So he
was crippled and overcome in order that he
should prevail, not by strength, but by supplica-
tion. Crippled, he could only hold on and plead
for the blessing. Yet it was God prevailing even
where Jacob prevailed, for He had so arranged it
that Jacob, in his defeat, should reap a greater
blessing.

[38]

Some of us have set out valiantly wrestling in our own power, and God has put us out of joint that, in our weakness, we might gain a greater victory than in our strength. It is in our weakness that His strength is made perfect. It is when we are maimed that we enter into fullest life.

If God has brought you to Jabbok, if you are up against a crisis alone and must meet your Esau, do not despair. It would appear that if ever Jacob needed to be in good trim, it was when he met Esau, and now he must meet him crippled! Ah, yes, but he is ten thousand times stronger, for now he is a Prince of God. So, do not try to wrestle through in your own power. God may have to put you out of joint to get you to the end of yourself, but then you can hold on in weakness and get the blessing. Give us more shrunken sinews, if they change us from Jacobs to Israels, to princes of God, and send us forth rejoicing that *"when we are weak, then are we strong!"*

GOD'S HAND

IN Old-Testament times Oriental servants were directed almost entirely by signs. Their part was to observe and obey. It is the true pose of the believer, utterly surrendered, watching, willing, working. God's eye is upon us: *"The eyes of the Lord are upon the righteous"* (Psa. 34:15). Our eyes must be turned toward Him, watching His hand.

And again, in Psalm 123:2, the Psalmist writes: *"Behold, as the eyes of servants look unto the hand of their masters, and as the eyes of a maiden unto the hand of her mistress; so our eyes wait upon the Lord our God, until that He have mercy upon us."*

His is a directing hand. *"It is not in man that walketh to direct his steps"* (Jer. 10:23), but *"in all thy ways acknowledge Him, and He shall direct thy paths"* (Prov. 3:6). As He led with pillar of cloud and pillar of fire, so He directs both the steps and the stops of those who wait upon Him.

His is a supplying hand. *"My God shall supply all your need according to His riches in glory by*

Christ Jesus" (Phil. 4:19). He supplies the wherewithal to carry out His directions. Someone said
to George Müller, "You must live from hand to
mouth." "I do," he returned, "but it's *God's*
hand." There will always be meal in the barrel
when we are in His will. He can feed with ravens
and spread tables in the wilderness. We grow
panicky, we worry over making a living. We forget that we are here only to do God's will, and that
our earthly business, our trade or occupation, is
simply to pay the expenses of doing His will. He
will supply the need His will creates.

Observe that His is a protecting hand. *"The
angel of the Lord encampeth round about them
that fear Him, and delivereth them"* (Psa. 34:7).
"We are immortal until our work is done." If we
are in His will, He will keep us here until that purpose is accomplished. There is no being killed pre-
maturely, dying too soon, if we are utterly in Him.
He keeps us, our real selves and lives, whatever
may happen to our bodies or bank-accounts, because they are hid with Christ in God.

Notice that His is a correcting hand. *"Whom
the Lord loveth He chasteneth, and scourgeth every
son whom He receiveth"* (Heb. 12:6). His correc-
tion is a mark of our sonship! If we had no chas-
tisement we should be bastards, and not sons. We
are wayward, and need it: *"Before I was afflicted I*

went astray: but now have I kept Thy word. . . .
It is good for me that I have been afflicted; that I
might learn Thy statutes" (Psa. 119:67, 71).

And, finally, look to His rewarding hand. *"A*
rewarder of them that diligently seek Him" (Heb.
11:6). The hand that directed and supplied knows
best how to reward. Men cannot rightly appraise
our lives. As Burns has put it:

> *"What's done we partly may compute,*
> *But know not what's resisted."*

Let us look to God's hand. I shall not forget
how Henry Barraclough watched Charles M. Alex-
ander as he played the piano under the great singer's direction. He did not watch the piano, but he
followed with his eye every move of his leader and
translated into music every shade of his interpretation. So we are not to observe ourselves or our
work or others, but look to God's great hand, waiting when He orders a halt, moving when He bids
us go, even though His directions seem sometimes
strange to us. It is not ours to reason and argue,
but simply to wait upon Him. So doing, we shall
be directed, supplied, protected, corrected—and
rewarded.

XII

"ONE THING—"

TO the rich young ruler Jesus said, "*One thing thou lackest.*" Money, position, morality, idealism, these were not enough. There is a goodness among moderns that is dangerous because so deceptive. It is the goodness of the young ruler. It is fine moral character, sincere and well-meaning, lit up with a desire to find life eternal. It frequently joins church, teaches a class, prays in public, is honest and aspiring. But it lacks one thing, and because of that tragic lack, its possessor goes away grieved when the real cost of discipleship is counted. We have a serious problem today in splendid men and women of sterling qualities who will not utterly renounce everything to follow Jesus in a life of faith. Their very virtues become hindrances because they count on them and ask, "What GOOD THING shall I do?" instead of forsaking their own poor righteousness, as did Paul his legal blamelessness, and counting only on the merits of Christ. To be sure, Jesus asked this young man to renounce his money, not his goodness; but the request showed up what sort of goodness he had. Promising qualities avail nothing if we are unwilling to *"hate father and mother,"* to forsake anything, however dear, that hinders the life of surrender and trust.

"But one thing is needful," said Jesus to the worried Martha. It is not a sit-down-and-do-nothing preachment. There must be practical Marthas in the kitchen. Notice the words, *"Martha was cumbered"*—*"Martha, Martha, thou art careful and troubled about many things."* He was not reprimanding her for working, He was gently reproving her for worrying. *"But one thing is needful—restful communion with Me."* We can commune with Him in the kitchen, but most of us are only cumbered, careful and anxious. Even in our practical Christian activities we become vexed and harassed. Our poor services will pass away, but contemplative communion with Him is that good part which shall not be taken away. Our sole business is to live in constant, abiding fellowship with Christ. If we become more interested in what we are doing for Christ than in what He is doing for us, we have reversed things and we shall end up as did Martha, cumbered instead of communing. But one thing is needful for the believer, to stay spiritually at His feet, hearing His word. Our hearts can sit at His feet while our hands work in the kitchen.

"This one thing I do," said Paul. He had found, long before, that there was one thing he lacked, and he tells us about it in this same chapter. He enumerates his good points before he knew Christ. It reminds us of the rich young ruler. He was blameless according to law-righteousness. Then he learned that there was one thing needful, *"the righteousness which is through the faith of Christ, the righteousness which is of God by faith."* Now that he has felt his lack and received the one thing needful, there is one more "one thing," and that is something to do. Nothing we can do will help until we have moved through these first two stages: then, there will be plenty to do. There is something to forget, *"those things which are behind"*; there is something to reach toward, *"those things which are before"*; there is something to press toward, *"the mark,"* the goal; there is something to work for, *"the prize of the high calling of God in Christ Jesus."*

Let these be the milestones of your spiritual experience: One thing I lack; one thing is needful; one thing I do.

XIII

THE GOD OF THE HOUSE OF GOD

WE are familiar with the story of Jacob's dream of the angels ascending and descending while he slept in a strange place with a stone pillow. That pillow became a pillar and Jacob called the place Bethel, the house of God.

Years later, after much sorrow and trouble, the Lord asks Jacob to return to Bethel, the place of blessing. He had been following a self-chosen way seeking prosperity. He had moved near Shechem and his daughter, Dinah, had gotten into society and into trouble. Jacob was distressed and, in his unhappiness, he reaped the harvest of misspent years. He had gained wealth, but he had lost much more; he had fallen out of close fellowship with the Lord; and he suffered the consequences of careless living. Like men today, he had figured from the standpoint of immediate and personal advantage, and had left out of consideration the spiritual involvements of each step he took.

So he makes a new start. He tells his household to put away strange gods, to be clean and change their garments. Would that fathers today would start in such a way for Bethel! There are some reading this who promised God years ago to be faithful, to trust and obey Him, come what might. But you have gotten out into the world, you have moved near Shechem, your family has moved into society and you have forgotten God. There will be no blessing for you until you return to Bethel. It costs too much in more ways than one to live at Shechem!

When Jacob returns to Bethel he calls it El-bethel (Gen. 35:7), "the God of the house of God." The first time the emphasis was on the place. Now he puts God first, and the emphasis is on the God of the place. The fellowship of God means more than any particular place or experience.

Some Christians make a fetish of rare moments and special experiences. They spend their time seeking spectacular spiritual thrills, mystic raptures, fine feelings. They like to set down dates that mean mountain-top days, astounding experiences. They are forever building tabernacles to house lofty visions and have no time to walk with the Lord day by day. Bethel is more important than El-bethel.

We ought always to value God Himself more highly than any event or occasion connected with our experience of Him. The knowledge of Christ day by day, in season and out· is life's true ideal.

Exalted moments do not last, and most of life is along the common road of the daily grind. But we can know Him in the tedious and commonplace, and so we shall if He is more to us than any special experience.

A man who had in his possession a precious ruby said to his friends, "Come down to my mill, and I will show you two very ordinary stones that bring in a better income than the ruby." He showed them two millstones, ugly and unattractive, but bringing in day by day a regular profit. Just so do the millstones of the daily grind bring us greater returns in the knowledge of Christ than the rubies of rare occasions.

Do not specialize in visions and special illuminations. He is more important than any place or event. We sing, "O Happy Day, That Fixed My Choice," and that is well, for there must be such a day if we are to know the Lord, but we must go on to "watch and pray, and live rejoicing every day." Like Philip, we ask to be shown the Father in some tremendous experience while God in Christ walks with us all the time and asks to be more fully recognized.

God is more important than His house, and we should ever put Him ahead of any deed or day associated with our experience of Him. El-bethel is better than Bethel.

XIV

"UNDERSTANDEST THOU?"

WHEN I was a student at Moody Bible Institute I was sent out once to play the piano for a service at a Swedish church. The entire service—songs, prayers and sermon—was rendered in Swedish and, although I played for the meeting, I did not understand one word that was uttered. I came away much impressed with the spiritual parallels of such an experience.

How many of us go through life, I reflected, taking a part, going through the perfunctory motions of living, yet never understanding the real message of existence, hearing voices, but knowing not what they say? The tragedy of passing the years hearing the sound, but deaf to the sense of the program of creation! Such men read great books, but only the words; the meaning is beyond them. They hear great music, but there is no message in the melody. They walk in the woods, but Nature's voice speaks unintelligible jargon. It is an awful thing to live like that, a mechanical automaton, acting a part but utterly ignorant of the play.

Some readers of the Bible are as much at home there as was I in the Swedish church. They go

[49]

through the act of reading so many words, so many verses, so many chapters. But, alas, the language is foreign, they know not what they read. It is the speech of another world, and one must be born into that world to understand the language.

Is it not so with the Church? Is it not one of our most pressing burdens that so many members of our churches sit through the service, perhaps taking a part, but utterly oblivious to the real message of sermon, prayer and song? They listen respectfully as I did to the Swedish service; they know that something good is going on; but it is the vernacular of another realm and beyond their comprehension.

We are not speaking of that lack of intellectual perception so often manifest when some scholarly speaker talks over the heads of an audience unable to rise to his academic phrases. We are thinking of that infinitely worse ignorance which may afflict the profoundest thinkers, the inability to understand the things of the Spirit. Here simplest people may have an understanding and shrewdest philosophers sit in the dark. How often does a lowly washerwoman follow every word of a discourse on things spiritual while a professor may stare blankly toward the pulpit in utter ignorance!

The Word has told us why this is so: *"The natural man receiveth not the things of the Spirit of God: for they are foolishness unto him: neither can*

[50]

*he know them, because they are spiritually dis-
cerned"* (1 Cor. 2:14). Here is a perception that
goes beyond all schools: for the lack of it the
learned sit in darkness and with it the humble see a
great light. It is open to all, the smart and the stu-
pid, but all who would have it must renounce the
wisdom of the world for *"the foolishness of God"*
(1 Cor. 1:25). Only those who have been born
again through faith in Jesus Christ can speak the
language of the redeemed or understand when it is
spoken. Mind you, I was sincere and active in the
Swedish service, BUT I UNDERSTOOD NOT.

At a gathering an aged minister and a famous
actor were present. The actor was asked to recite
and, at the minister's request, repeated the Twenty-
third Psalm. He rendered it charmingly and a mur-
mur of praise went around the assembly at the
close. Then the actor asked the old minister to repeat the Psalm. When the minister had ended there
were tears in all eyes, for he had uttered it from his
heart, with spiritual understanding. No one felt the
difference more keenly than the actor. "I know the
Psalm," he said, "but you know the Shepherd."

It is a tragic thing to know the Psalm and not the
Shepherd. Neither wealth nor wit nor will can
initiate you into the knowledge of the things of
the Spirit. *"They are spiritually discerned." "Ye
must be born again."*

[51]

XV

A MORNING CONCERT

IT is now officially springtime. The wood-
thrush has returned and stamped it with his
approval. I heard him this morning in an early
recital. I stood beside a stretch of calmest water
unruffled by even the faintest breeze. Beyond rose
the deep woods and from the edge of the moss-
hung cypresses the clear call of the feathered flutist
was borne across the little lake to me.

It was a perfect setting and the serene singer was
at his best. There is something about such moments, the holy quietness, the cadences of that
woodland voice, the tonic freshness of springtime,
that sets one's soul longing for a world untainted
by sordidness and sin. One catches a passing
glimpse of what this earth once was like before the
blight of death and corruption and yearns to escape
from the absurd nightmare of modernity to some
restful haven where the delirium tremens of "progress" has not come.

Near-by where I stood baby-ducks paddled in the
water. High overhead I caught the note of passing
wild geese and looked in time to see them, faintly

visible, a happy brigade homeward bound. On all sides arose the tumult of new voices, the cardinal, the water thrush, the yellow-throat, the vireo, the warblers. In a world even as broken and bruised as it is today, there are many reminders of a blessed harmony still to come. These interludes of loveliness are not tantalizing jests of an ironical fate, brighter moments of a maniac universe bound for oblivion. Paradise shall be restored!

The wood-thrush has begun again. The best part of his song escapes when one tries to set it down in words, but there is an elusive something in the lilt of those tones that brings back memories of carefree days long passed. A ragged country youngster who stayed in the woods with his shepherd dog; high dreams of youth and lofty visions; happy summer days in sylvan solitudes, the woods his fairyland, bird and butterfly his elves and sprites. Hard reality and the stern necessities of this artifical age have toned down the calliope notes of youth, but in such rare moments we escape the modern grind while the wood-thrush turns backward old Time in his flight.

But in these later years we have learned to rejoice in a blessed truth of the Book. We cannot believe that the loveliness of Nature is doomed to extinction. We believe that *"the whole creation groaneth and travaileth in pain together until now,"*

waiting *"for the manifestation of the sons of God."*
As man sings amid his troubles in hope of a better
world we like to think the song of the wood-thrush
is an expression of a longing creation yearning for
a redeemed earth. Instead of losing our hope for a
land of pure delight in the midst of this matter-
minded world, we grow daily more confident of
reaching through our Lord the new Paradise, where
"the wolf also shall dwell with the lamb."

How tragic that men have so lost themselves in
the modern scramble for a life that consisteth in
the abundance of the things one possesseth that
these intimations of a better world fall on ears
utterly deafened! How many ever hear the message of the wood-thrush? If ever they go to the
woods it is to slay and kill. If they hear a bird it
is a caged canary! No wonder we have grown so
dry and destitute.

Shut off your radio and attend a woodland con-
cert. Deep will call unto deep, and if you listen in
the light of His Word you shall hear things high
and holy.

XVI

WHEN "THE GOOD DIE YOUNG"

ONCE in a while someone raises the old problem about the death of, let us say, David Blank. He was a fine and promising young preacher, just through school and ready to begin what undoubtedly would have been a most fruitful ministry. Suddenly death takes him and the sceptics begin the familiar barrage of puzzlers: "Why did God take such a useful young man when He needs preachers so much and when there are so many worthless characters hanging around who ought to die? It's a strange Providence. It looks more like pure chance and happen-so."

Such argument proceeds, of course, from the foolish assumption that this world is the whole show. If things don't turn out here as it seems they should, why they never will! It is the philosophy of earth-bound mortals who don't take eternity into consideration. They fail to see that this earth is only a conditioning ground for the life beyond and that David Blank is better prepared for the next chapter of his eternal career exactly because he studied and prepared and was a good man.

If everything ended with death, even then it would be better to go as David went, but when you reflect that he is still living it is clear that he laboured not in vain.

God's Word tells us that the next life, or rather the continued life of the Christian in the state after death, is one of activity. We do not sit on clouds strumming harps through all eternity. We read of the glorified saints in Revelation 7:15: *"Therefore are they before the throne of God, and serve Him day and night in His temple: and He that sitteth on the throne shall dwell among them."* We read further in Revelation 22:3, in the glorious passage about the final Paradise: *"And there shall be no more curse: but the throne of God and of the Lamb shall be in it;* AND HIS SERVANTS SHALL SERVE HIM." Do you not think David Blank is all the better fitted for that continued service? Was not the servant who had been faithful over a few things made ruler over many (Matt. 25:21, 23)? Was not the servant who had used well his ten pounds given authority over ten cities and the five-pound steward given five cities? David Blank invested well what he had while he could. God asks no more of any servant.

There is a further thought. God is not so much interested in how long we live or in how much we do, as in our willingness to do. He found out that

David Blank meant business, and that was enough. The supreme thing in any life is not the quantity of work done: it is not how many sermons have been preached nor how many songs sung or good deeds done. It is a matter of whether we were willing to do as long as we could. With some, God gives them a long time to prove willingness by work. With others, He accepts the will for the deed and carries them on into the next world to serve Him there.

Whichever way He takes with you or me, rest assured that we never waste any time that is spent in preparing better to do His will. We are serving Him as truly while we train as when we actually go to the battle. In fact, all of this life is but a training, anyway, for real service to come.

Do not forget that Jesus trained thirty years for only three years of public service. No, David Blank was not cut off too soon. God has more for him to do. God cares more for the love of the servant than the length of the service. David proved his love as far as he went. God is more interested in the quality of the doer than in the quantity of the deeds. David Blank, like Enoch, walked with God, and God took him.

It is not, How much did you work? or, How long did you work? but, Were you willing to work? and, Did you work as long as you could?

XVII

A PASTOR'S REVERY

I HAVE just conducted the burial service of a tiny baby. It is one of those tender duties which a pastor stores among his precious memories. Simple and brief, yet it contains all those basic elements of love and grief and death and the hope of a life to come. The life of a country preacher may seem humdrum to the thrill-chaser of earth, but, dealing as it does with life's deepest realities, it is inestimably rich in treasures dug from the mine of human experience.

This little burial was a common event, happening every day somewhere, but woe unto the minister who sees in it but a part of his routine. As we stood at the tiny grave, only a few friends, the young father and mother, and a sweet baby-sister, and a coloured helper whose own father and mother recently had died, I was deeply touched with the tender simplicity of it all. Here were love and heartache, friendliness and sympathy, the old, old agony of separation and the dear hope of a reunion to come.

I read the familiar account of the death of

David's child and how he said, *"I shall go to him, but he will not return to me."* The young wife sobbed upon the shoulder of a sturdy husband and friends bowed with that silent sympathy which words would spoil. The little sister cried, not comprehending, of course, for she was equally as gleeful when I carried her to the store for some candy. Somehow the little scene seemed to sum up the broad outlines of life's little story: we are born, we love, we marry, we bow in grief as tenderest cords snap, and the plain, kindly old earth receives us again.

A sophisticated modern world has grown too smart rightly to value these elemental things. Love has been "debunked," marriage has become a temporary convenience, children have become nuisances and the tender fundamentals of old-fashioned family life have been thrown overboard. Religion has been ignored and death is increasingly regarded the end of an ironic joke. Having sown the wind, we now reap the whirlwind, and if it were not for those simpler souls to whom these holy ties are sacred this world would be a madhouse.

We have developed a complicated and bewildering programme of living, and have lost ourselves in a multitude of things when but few things are needful. To grow, to love, to work, to share the common lot of joy and sorrow; to know the elemental experiences of our existence glorified by faith in God through Jesus Christ; to accept life without trying to explain it; to come to grips with its realities and not dodge them in a masquerade of make-believe; to come to die and hold "we sleep to wake"—that is enough.

So these common experiences of the pastor serve to keep us face to face with life as it is. They save us from vaporous theorizing and demand that we bear a message that can actually meet the daily need. I think the Lord Jesus spent so much of His precious time on earth meeting the practical problems of obscure people partly to teach us that the world does not need our theories, but rather our faith and love and service in the daily grind. Far better than the tongues of men and angels is the love that suffers long and is kind. Better than a clever metaphysical discourse is a message that can soothe aching hearts at a baby's grave.

XVIII

GOOD NEWS FROM A FAR COUNTRY

WE believers are pilgrims in a strange land. We look for a city, we seek a country, we desire a better country, that is, an heavenly (Heb. 11:10, 14, 16). Our citizenship is in heaven (Phil. 3:20). Throughout our earthly sojourn we are privileged to hear from our eternal home, and *"as cold waters to a thirsty soul, so is good news from a far country"* (Prov. 25:25).

It may come in the hour of prayer, in the calm of meditation, through a good sermon, a spiritual book, conversation with a friend. Many are the messengers that bring us tidings from afar. Sometimes they come gay and radiant, and sometimes they wear black. But every bearer should be welcomed, even through tears, if he bears good news from God's country.

I have a book of letters from the far country. Over half of it is filled with messages made known through angels and men of God. Then a heavenly host announces, *"Fear not: for, behold, I bring you good tidings of great joy, which shall be to all peo-*

[61]

ple. For unto you is born this day in the city of David a Saviour, which is Christ the Lord." That is the Gospel which means simply Good News. Then there came One Who announced Himself as the fulfilment of all prophecy before Him and Who brought the message of the kingdom of God. When they killed Him He arose to bring good news of victory over death. And finally He returned to an old disciple on lonely Patmos to show Himself glorified and triumphant.

Through this good Book I learn that God loves me; that Jesus died for me; that whosoever believes on Him shall not perish, but have everlasting life. I learn that if I believe in Him He pleads my cause before the Father; that He indwells me; that through Him I can reign in life. I find that death is not the end; that He is coming to earth again; that I shall live forever with Him in glory. As cold waters to a thirsty soul, so is such good news from a far country.

This good news, this Gospel, is for every one. It reaches in every direction like the very word "news," N for north, E for east, W for west, and S for south. It is the power of God unto salvation to every one that believeth.

You and I can bear this good news, for there is a "Gospel According to You and Me." We are epistles of Christ (2 Cor. 3:3). The world reads us more closely than it does the Bible. Do we relay good news from God? If so, we, too, shall be as cold water to thirsty souls. *"The water that I shall give him shall be in him a well of water springing up into everlasting life"* (Jno. 4:14).

Men like to read news and the printing-presses grind out tons of it each morning. But not much of it is good news, and far less is good news from the Far Country. Is it not strange that, while in each home lies a Bible with news from heaven, men let dust gather upon it from week to week while they peruse the county paper!

Good news from a far country! Brother, do you read it? Do you heed it? Do you speed it to others?

XIX

LAZY

IT is a lazy day in the lowlands. I sit, half-asleep, by the window. In the lilacs just outside a yellow warbler plays like a golden sprite and somewhere in the shade-tree beyond a catbird sings a subdued medley. There's a yellow-throat in the hedge across the road and a humming-bird zooms among the sweet-williams. It is a dreamy day in this leisurely land of heron and herring.

Some "darkies" are picking blackberries near-by. Of course there is plenty of fun and frolic there. These children of Ham haunt me with their simple life and philosophy. The white man thinks himself superior, but are they poorer than we? Born in poverty, nurtured in adversity, inured to want and scantiness, have they not garnered from hardship a wisdom which we have lost in the maze of "progress"? Their simple faith and perennial good cheer shame men who have gained the world and lost their souls.

One of them, a tiny mite of a pickaninny, has come across to sing for a penny. He sang, "I'm Sitting on Top of the World," and I think he is!

At least he is nearer the summit than some million-aire trying to forget his indigestion on a golf course. He has health and innocence and happiness, and the Saviour used such as he for a model. Strange are the ways of life that men sweat and spend and strive to reach what some darky picking black-berries already has!

Recently I went to one of their humble cabins to pray with a very old negro man, who lay at the door of death. I was touched by the sweet sim-plicity of the roomful of coloured friends who knelt with me in prayer. Such gentle, unquestioning faith in the Heavenly Father which many reach only after miserable years! Why do not more of us so trust Him at the outset and save all the agony of roundabout ways? We must come to it, any-way, or to despair!

I have been back by the waterside this morning. Like a flawless mirror the wide creek reflects the cypresses on the other side. I heard Parula warb-lers and saw a mother wild duck leading her pretty little brood in a paddle across to the lily-fringed swamp-edge. There was something so calm and soothing about it all that I felt I should like to live right on that shore for ages.

Nothing is more delightful than to drift along these still waterways late in the afternoon. In al-most every little nook or inlet one may spy somebody idly fishing, for such afternoons lure many others beside myself away from work they are supposed to do! Somehow the fevers and frets of this ballyhoo age blow away in such retreats and the overrated enthusiasms we are frenzied over shrink down to their pitiful actual size. It is a good place to go to laugh at oneself for letting the times make such a clown of him.

I am glad the Word pictures for me a river of life and a tree of life in the Paradise of God (Rev. 22:1-5). I cannot imagine a heavenly life that does not include a glorified counterpart to this lovely world of trees and streams. And if a lazy loitering along these waterways can so exalt the soul, what must await us over there!

XX

A DEEP, SETTLED PEACE

IT was a little service on a cold February night, held in a renovated old schoolhouse, with a small attendance of humble, farming folk. One woman had started on foot for the service, which which was seven miles from her home, and had been picked up and brought on by a merciful passer-by. We held a short testimony service and several told of what the Lord had done for their souls. The last to speak was a humble woman, plainly dressed, who rose quietly and gave a witness I shall not forget. "I praise the Lord," she said, "for a deep, settled peace. The world did not give it to me, and the world can't take it away."

That testimony lingers with me. I think of scholars and sages ransacking libraries and perusing heavy philosophies, searching for the secret of peace, while the plain, farm-woman has been enjoying it through the years. I think of those who eagerly frequent doctor and saint, looking for the magic key, the "open sesame" to rest and serenity, and all the while this simple soul has lived in the secret of His Presence. Verily He has kept these

things from the wise and prudent and revealed them
unto babes. Truly not many mighty, wise and
noble have been called. God hath chosen the weak,
base, foolish things and things which are not.
There are thousands of earth's rich and renowned
who would give it all for the childish confidence of
the soul that on Jesus hath leaned for repose—if
only they could get it their way!

The poor and plain have no monopoly on the
things of the spirit, but usually I have found the
sweetest peace among them. I think of an old
negro who runs a little bootblack stand in a hotel.
Certainly that is hardly a congenial place to grow
placidity of spirit, but he has done it. The peace
of God which passes knowledge garrisons his heart.
I know a farmer in the hills who, while the world
has hurried past him, has taken time to be holy, to
be calm in his soul. In the presence of such humble saints our little shop-talk becomes absurd, they
speak another language from the efficient, snappy,
sophisticated jargon of this insane age. Their com-
pany seems to breathe a fragrance as of a better
world, something sweet and precious like old letters
and old songs. How superficial our smartness becomes before the gentle wisdom of these strange
pilgrims whose secret souls a holier strain repeat!

How blessed are they who know this deep, settled peace which the world cannot give nor take

away! *"My peace I give unto you; not as the world giveth, give I unto you."* It lifts us above the tedium of drudgery, the bondage of circumstance. We know that all things work together for good to us, that God will supply our need, that our life is hid with Christ in God. We do not fret about self-preservation, for we know "we are immortal until our work is done." We may live from hand to mouth, but it is God's hand. *"Great peace have they who love Thy law, and nothing shall offend them."*

It is blessed so to live, and if we so live the going will be pleasant.

> *"Lord, grant me if Thou wilt,*
> *To slip away*
> *As slips the night into the dawning day;*
> *So soft that e'en the watchers, watching,*
> *Cannot say, Here ends the night,*
> *And here begins the day,*
> *But only know the night's Thy night,*
> *The day Thy day."*

XXI

THE YAKIMA AND YOU

I SPENT a little while in the apple-paradise of the
Yakima Valley, in the State of Washington.
What was once a waste of sand and sagebrush
has been reclaimed and transformed into priceless
orchards. Barrenness has become bounty; the
desert blossoms as the rose.

I have strolled leisurely along the winding roads
that creep through the fruitful domains. At even-
tide I liked to sit atop one of these rocky buttes and
watch the sun sink back of the near-by mountains
that stand so gaunt and barren and cold. For even
in October, although the days grow warm, the
nightfall calls to the fireside and bedtime calls for
blankets thick and warm.

Irrigation has wrought its miracle here. I have
always been deeply interested in whatever means
salvage, reclamation, transformation. There is a
school of thought today which makes the tree to be
forever inclined as the twig is bent. Its god is circumstance and from environment it knows no re-
demption. But if science can make cacti edible and
turn deserts into gardens, it is childishly irrational

[70]

to deny the Creator to do with His creatures what the creature can do with lower orders of life. There are human lives as desolate as the arid stretches of New Mexico or Nevada that floods of His redemptive grace can make into groves and gardens of blessing.

"Down in the human heart, crushed by the tempter,
Feelings lie buried that grace can restore;
Touched by a loving hand, wakened by kindness,
Chords that were broken will vibrate once more."

Where sin did abound, grace can and will much more abound. If we abide in Him we shall bring forth much fruit. Men can transform malarial swamps into health resorts. And God can take foul and stagnant lives, ridden with the fevers and filth of sin, and make them paradises of His Presence, lit with His sunlight, watered with the Eternal Springs, cooled with the breezes from heavenly altitudes.

While Nehemiah rebuilt Jerusalem's walls we read that Sanballat mockingly enquired, *"Will they revive the stones out of the heaps of the rubbish?"* (Neh. 4:2). A revival from rubbish! It seemed absurd. So it seems today to the wordly outsiders. The modern Sanballats tell us that men cannot be transformed; rubbish must stay rubbish; garbage cannot become gardens. But God has been building walls from waste these centuries. What a rocky prospect was Simon Peter! What barrenness was Paul and Augustine and Jerry McCauley! What continents of blight He has made into beauty!

What is true of the Yakima may be true with you. Your desolation may become delight. Yield the waste-lands of your heart to the Heavenly Husbandman. And *"you shall go out with joy, and be led forth with peace: the mountains and the hills shall break forth before you into singing, and all the trees of the field shall clap their hands. Instead of the thorn shall come up the fir tree, and instead of the brier shall come up the myrtle tree: and it shall be to the Lord for a name, for an everlasting sign that shall not be cut off."*

For the righteous man *"shall be like a tree planted by the rivers of water, that bringeth forth his fruit in his season; his leaf also shall not wither; and whatsoever he doeth shall prosper."*

God can make things over, whether with the Yakima or you!

XXII

"THE WELL IS DEEP"

THE woman at Jacob's well was measuring the Lord by circumstances. *"Thou hast nothing to draw with,"* she said, *"and the well is deep"* (Jno. 4:11).

It is a common failing of weak believers. The Word is filled with rich and radiant promises of power through the Spirit. God waits to do wonders in our lives. But we see only the well of circumstance. "Ah, yes, it is all very wonderful to live by faith, I suppose. It may do for the minister and others who are better fitted for it, but really it won't work in my case. It sounds very well in the pulpit and in devotional books and in the hymns, but with a disposition like mine or a humdrum job such as I'm sentenced to, or with a provoking family like mine—the well is too deep, I fear."

You see what that amounts to, it is simply doubting God. It is accusing Him of favoritism if His Spirit is adaptable only to a few. Moreover, it makes Him to lie if it won't work in any circumstance when He has promised the Spirit to all who

[73]

ask Him. Yet we deliberately go pointing at our wells: "He has nothing to draw with; He cannot overcome such limitations as there are in my case."

The woman at the well went on to say (v. 12): *"Art Thou greater than our father Jacob, which gave us the well, and drank thereof himself, and his children, and his cattle?"* Is Jesus greater than Jacob! We measure our lives by the things we get from Jacob, the things which come to us by natural descent and by ordinary circumstance. "All I have I got by my wits and hard work: this talk about faith and higher power is out of my range." But there is One greater than Jacob. There is a higher resource than the natural assets of life. There is a better well than Jacob's.

Yes, most believers, while they believe theoretically in the Spirit, live their lives at Jacob's well. Each of us has a way of thinking his trouble must be just a bit peculiar: "Yes, the Lord can overcome that, but now my difficulty is different." We look at ourselves and measure Him by our own weakness. "He cannot get any water out of such a life as mine." He is not going to; He never draws power out of us, He puts power into us from above. "I am so weak." Well, He never promised to do wonders with our weakness, but by His strength.

So we insist on thinking our case is a little too

hard for the Lord. "I know my temper." "I know I shouldn't do this, but a man must live, and God isn't going to pay my bills." Then we offer the pious excuse that we are not doubting Christ, that we are doubting ourselves. We get down in the wells of our own pitiful resources, trying to dip up strength when He has offered to supply our needs.

Beware of looking at yourself and then wondering how God can do things with you. The water He offers does not come from your well. He is not going to draw His power from your reservoir. You must learn that there is a Divine Well springing from above that has nothing to do with your little resources, the well that Jacob left you, your natural endowments and reserves. So long as we think the Christian life is a cultivation of the old nature, a mere improvement of the old well, we shall never know His living water springing up in us to everlasting life. He is not asking to dig deeper in the well of your life nor to sweeten the waters there. He wants to lead you to a new well.

By which well are you living: the well of Jacob or the well of Jesus?

XXIII

THE CRISES OF ABRAHAM

AS one studies the life of Abraham, the man of faith, he is impressed with several crises in his spiritual experience each of which brought him to a closer walk with God. Each required a surrender and each surrender brought a blessing.

The first (Gen. 12:1-3) called him to leave his country, kindred and father's house to journey by faith in a strange land. In Heb. 11:8 we read: *"By faith Abraham, when he was called to go out into a place which he should after receive for an inheritance, obeyed; and he went out, not knowing whither he went."* God often calls us to forsake close ties to walk by faith in strange places, but if we obey we shall afterward receive those places, as did Abraham, for an inheritance. Jesus Christ issued such a challenge (Matt. 10:34-37, Luke 14:26).

Again, Abraham reached a crisis when it became necessary for him to separate from Lot. He loved Lot and probably had thought of him as an heir. But Lot, though a believer, was not a consecrated

[76]

man, and God in His wisdom brings about a separation (Gen. 13:5-11). It must have been a disappointment to Abraham. In Genesis 15:1-3 we find him reduced to the prospect of his steward Eliezer becoming his heir. Sometimes God reduces us until our only prospect is an Eliezer, but He has blessings in store when we obey, as He revealed to Abraham (Gen. 13:14-18 and 15:4-21). All he saw was his, with the promise of progeny as numerous as the stars!

Then Abraham had to give up his own preferences and plans about Ishmael. Ishmael was born out of the will of God for Abraham, who had taken the way of flesh instead of the way of faith to provide himself an heir (Gen. 16:1-6). As always, this brought on trouble. Abraham wished that Ishmael might live before God (Gen. 17:18, 19), but God had other plans. Often we want our Ishmaels, our own selfish arrangements and projects, to succeed, but God wants us to fail in ourselves, that we might find the blessing not in the deeds of the flesh, but through faith. Our Ishmaels must fail that our Isaacs may succeed.

Finally God called for the sacrifice of Isaac, the son of faith. Ishmael represented the worst thing in Abraham's life, and God took him away and he never came back. Isaac was the best thing in Abraham's life, so God took him but gave him

[77]

back. It is so in His dealings with you and me. God wants the Ishmaels that He may utterly remove them; the Isaacs that He may restore them to us like Moses' rod, a double blessing. After this great surrender of Abraham's God came to him with great assurance (Gen. 22:15-18). Real victory in things spiritual always follows genuine surrender.

Abraham's progress was gradual. He did not learn it all at once. For instance, twice he was involved in lying about Sarah (Gen. 12 and 20). A peculiarity about this lie was, it was a half-truth: Sarah was his half-sister (Gen. 20:12). But God dealt with it as a lie because it was told with the intention to deceive.

The development of Abraham required time and testing. While the Christian experience is not, primarily, a matter of giving up things, such crises do bring us to the end of self and cut off all outside interests that our faith might be utterly in God.

XXIV

KNOWING THE BIBLE "BY HEART"

IT was a series of religious services for which a very learned preacher had been imported as the star speaker. The opening devotionals were, as usual, given to relatively obscure local ministers. But the academic address went clear over our heads while a simple pastor of a back-street church touched our hearts with a few plain words.

I came away reflecting that there is a deeper understanding of the Word found often among humblest folk untaught in schools, a clearer perception of things spiritual, which cultured scholars often utterly miss. The Bible is not like other books. The best approach to the understanding of it is not by head but by heart. Greek and Hebrew, exegesis and theology, these do not necessarily open to us the Scriptures in their truest light. There is sometimes a tendency among seminary graduates to look down upon Bible students who have studied only the English Bible by the help of the Spirit. Now the Holy Spirit is the best interpreter of His own Book, and to the humble searcher who would hide the Word in his heart and not merely in his head great things are revealed. *"Eye hath not seen, nor ear heard, neither have entered into the heart of man the things which God hath prepared for them that love Him. But God hath revealed them unto us by His Spirit"* (1 Cor. 2:9, 10). That principle applies to the study of the Word.

Indeed, if the Bible's message were so hidden that only scholars and seminary students could find it most of us believers would be hopelessly in the dark. It is part of the miracle of the Book that God has prepared it so that it unfolds itself to the simplest souls and not merely to intellectual investigation. Of course, academic training should help, and does when rightly combined with other preparation still more valuable. No person need feel discouraged over lack of theological education, for there is an understanding of the Word which is utterly independent of scholarship and open to the unschooled as freely as to the learned.

We fill our libraries with books about the Bible, and some of us need to learn the truth expressed by the old coloured preacher. He had borrowed a commentary from a white preacher and, upon returning it, was asked what he thought of it. He replied that the Bible certainly did throw a lot of light on it! Dr. Campbell Morgan laid aside his books and for years studied only the Bible. The Book is its own best expositor.

When men approach the Bible from any principle of study and interpretation except the principle laid down in the Scriptures, the end is always confusion. For the Bible is not an ordinary book, it moves in another realm, and its laws are the laws of that realm. Spiritual preparation and prayerful study unlock its treasures. That is why the pastor of the back-street church may excel the scholarly star preacher.

There is a wisdom in *"the foolishness of God"* greater than the wisdom of men. There is a wisdom of spiritual perception among humble believers that is greater than the wisdom of learned Christians who are hiding the Word in their heads and not storing it in their hearts. We speak of "knowing the Bible by heart" when we mean "by memory." One may know *all* by memory, and not know it by heart.

XXV

"THERE IS YET ONE MAN—"

I AM impressed with the conduct of Micaiah, the prophet, as recorded in 1 Kings 22. Ahab and Jehoshaphat have allied in their own strength to wage war against Syria. Jehoshaphat proposes that the mind of God first be ascertained, and Ahab summons four hundred false prophets who glibly advise him, *"Go up; for the Lord shall deliver it* [Ramoth-Gilead] *into the hand of the king."* We still have professional Pollyannas, opportunists, and time-servers, who preach the popular thing, prophesying peace when there is no peace. One hears in these dark days a false optimism from many pulpits endorsing the world's vain policies and bidding Ahab go up to Ramoth-Gilead.

Jehoshaphat does not seem to have been satisfied with this gushing outburst, no doubt sensing its superficiality. He enquires, *"Is there not here a prophet of the Lord besides, that we might enquire of him?"* Ahab's reply is significant: *"There is yet one man, Micaiah the son of Imlah, by whom we may enquire of the Lord: but I hate him, for he*

[82]

doth not prophesy good concerning me, but evil."
God's preacher is not popular. They hate him who
rebukes in the gate and abhor him who speaks up-
rightly (Amos 5:10).

But Micaiah is sent for, and meanwhile the kings
sit in state and the false prophets wax eloquent, for
rarely may one preach before two kings! Zedekiah
adds a touch of the dramatic and illustrates his
message with two horns, a theatrical flourish which
must have been ludicrous indeed. A chance to address royalty doubtless makes fools of most prophets. Paul before Agrippa is another story.

The messenger sent to Micaiah advises him to
fall in line with the other prophets and prophesy
smooth things. It is the old urge to follow the
crowd, harmonize with the spirit of the times.
Micaiah meets it majestically: *"What the Lord
saith unto me, that will I speak."* Here is a man
who really is different.

So he goes to the king and, at first in ironical
mockery of the false prophets, bids the king go to
battle. Then he declares in plainest terms that the
battle will be a failure and that the prophets are
liars. That was a blow for Zedekiah the dramatic;
he smites the prophet and asks, *"Which way went
the spirit of the Lord from me to speak to thee?"*
It is a biting and bitter attack, but Micaiah meets
it with another prophecy: *"Behold, thou shalt see*

in that day, when thou shalt go into an inner chamber to hide thyself." "You will find out when you are trying to hide!"

The king sends Micaiah to prison with hard fare prescribed, bread and water of affliction. True prophets are not always rewarded with an increase in salary and a church downtown. Many of God's Micaiahs still eat his fare.

That does not upset the rugged seer. The king has commanded that he be kept in prison, *"until I return in peace."* Micaiah uses the phrase for a parting prophecy: *"If thou return at all in peace, the Lord hath not spoken by me"*; then he bids everybody pay attention to what he has said.

There is a magnificence about this man who towers above the manikins of this chapter like Gulliver above the Lilliputians. It is good to know that in such an age when preachers were but clowns at court that *"there was yet one man"* to whom kings meant nothing, who would tell the truth at any cost. It is so easy to boost the popular enthusiasms, to take advantage of passing sentiment and advertise one's self as did Zedekiah on the bandwagon of a current fad. Blessed is the exception who will spoil the fun with the truth from God and go to his bread and water of affliction having kept the faith.

XXVI

"A CLOUD LIKE A MAN'S HAND"

AFTER the amazing miracle on Carmel, Elijah bids Ahab get up, eat and drink, for there is a sound of abundance of rain—the long drought is about to be broken. There is yet no sign in the sky, but Elijah speaks in faith. Then, the prophet goes up on top of Carmel and casts himself upon the ground, putting his face between his knees. He bids his servant go look toward the sea for a sign of rain. The servant goes, but sees nothing. Elijah bids him go seven times, and with the seventh trip comes the report, *"Behold, there ariseth a little cloud out of the sea, like a man's hand"* (1 Kings 18:44). Elijah immediately sends word to Ahab and starts toward Jezreel.

Here are significant truths for us. Elijah lives in confidence that there will be rain. At the proper time, he is in contrition, his head between his knees. He uses common sense, bidding his servant look toward the sea where the cloud would be most likely to arise. He is not disappointed with the first report, but sends the servant back seven times in patient continuance. Most of us give up and go down the Carmel of prayer when the first report shows no sign of rain! Naaman must wash seven times. The child of the Shunammite, whom Elisha restored, sneezed seven times. Jesus bids us forgive a brother seven times a day if he so offend us. We need to learn the lesson of God's sevens.

Finally comes the report of the little cloud like a man's hand, and Elijah acted upon it immediately. God often answers us with a little cloud like a man's hand, and we do not act upon so small a prospect because we want something stupendous and spectacular to happen. We are not willing to fare forth upon the encouragement of a little cloud; we want the thunder and lightnings of some dramatic manifestation. Consequently, there are no showers of blessing.

Moody and Sankey undertook their first evangelistic mission to England upon the invitation of two rather obscure men. One of them had died when they arrived. Their first meeting was attended by a bare handful. It was truly a cloud like a man's hand. But they did not leave Carmel in disgust; they moved forward in faith until God sent a downpour of the Spirit in the land.

Some of us still are huddled on Carmel, our heads between our knees, waiting for more assurance, when we ought to girdle up our loins and be on our way toward Jezreel. We read that when Elijah acted upon the report, *"The hand of the Lord was on Elijah"* (v. 46). They that wait on the Lord shall run and not be weary, and the prophet was enabled to run this course because he had waited. But remember that we are not to wait all the time: when the cloud rises it is time to run.

God does not answer always with dazzling, tremendous certainties. Sometimes He comes, not with earthquake and wind and fire, but with the still, small voice. Sometimes the answer is not encouraging, it is only a little cloud, but He means for us to act upon it. Are we willing to take the cloud for the rain and count Him faithful Who has promised? We want too much guaranteed in advance, we forget that faith is the substance of things hoped for, the evidence of things not seen. God does not spoil us by granting too much at a time: He tries us with a little cloud to see whether we start for Jezreel or stay on Carmel.

Do not run before the Lord and take matters into your own hands before you see the cloud. But when it arises, gird up your loins and set out running. The hand of the Lord shall be upon you; you shall run and not be weary.

XXVII

THE DISCIPLE WHO STAYED AT HOME

THE Gadarene demoniac, now clothed and in his right mind, begs to go along with Jesus (Mark 5:18). It must have looked romantic and alluring, the Lord and His disciples boarding the ship to cross over the little sea to new places and more adventures. The new disciple wanted to get away from old familiar territory, the scene of his horrible past, and begin anew elsewhere. How interesting to go here and there with this wonderful band and testify in strange places! Above all, he wanted to spend his life with the One Who had saved him from such a living terror and had made him a new creature. What disciple would not beg to get away from Gadara and go along with Jesus!

But it is not to be. Instead, Jesus bids him, *"Go home to thy friends, and tell them how great things the Lord hath done for thee, and hath had compassion on thee"* (v. 19). It is not a very glamorous commission and it might have disappointed some souls. "Go back to the old familiar and unromantic grounds where you have been such a hideous character and live down that past, overcome it by your new testimony. Don't run away from Gadara, stay right there and live for Me as earnestly as once you did for the devil. It will be hard, for everybody knows what you have been: they will call you names, and some will be slow to believe you, and others will call you a freak, but there is your mission field, you must be My disciple who stayed at home."

Do you grow weary of Gadara and long to break away to more alluring adventures across the sea? It is a glorious thing to follow the Christ to far lands and strange places. But I am thinking that sometimes it is even nobler to give up fond dreams of high endeavour in more romantic climes and go back home to live down a black past, proclaiming in dull and difficult circumstances what God has done for one's soul. All of us are smitten with that urge to cross over to better places: "If only I were yonder, how I could preach!" But only a few ever go, and sometimes it is not so romantic on the other side when they get there. Most of us cannot take passage for exciting service beyond the sea. We shall have to stay in Gadara and testify at home.

Of course, the Gadarene wanted most just to be with Jesus. What a beautiful evidence of a new affection that he does not want the Saviour even to get out of sight! But more blessed are they who see not, yet believe. Greater it is to labour on in Decapolis, walking by faith and not by sight, than to walk in His bodily presence three years like Peter or Judas, then deny or betray Him! Do not give much importance to fine experiences of sense and feeling: better be instant in season and out, feel like it or not.

"There is Preacher Blank. I wonder why he stuck to those country churches in the mountains. He was pretty rough back in other days when he grew up in that community. Then he was saved and went off to school. Nobody thought he would ever come back to that country, for he was smart and able, and we thought he would land in a city pulpit. But he turned down several chances and stayed in the backwoods, built up churches, lived down the past and turned many to righteousness."

Haven't you heard that once in a while? We have an idea that such Preacher Blanks maybe knew a day when they cast a long, eager look toward the sea, toward far lands and distant horizons. But the ship pulled away without them, while they turned back to commonplace sights in familiar old Gadara. For it is not given to all men to go with the ship to fields of fine romance. There must be the disciple who stayed at home to tell his friends what the Lord had done for his soul.

XXVIII

GOD'S POST-OFFICE

OUR post-office is a dull and commonplace affair, viewed from without by the un-interested passer-by. One would hardly connect it with anything thrilling or romantic. Just a little wired cage, a few boxes, a desk and a table—can anything worth while come through that little window from such a plain and unpoetic corner of a country store?

Indeed there can! Through that little window have come messages that have sent me fairly skipping down the road, gleeful as a farm-boy on his first spring fishing trip. It has relayed to me letters which have fairly changed the course of my career. And from that very ordinary post-office have come missives that have saddened my soul.

Really there are few places on earth more charged with human interest than a post-office. Have you ever thought how packed with joy and sorrow, despair and delight, one ugly mail-bag may be? Have you reflected how one day's batch of letters may file out through that little window to prosper some and pauperize others, lead this man to marriage and that to murder, kill here and cure there? I've almost decided our little old post-office is the most romantic place of all!

But the post-office is not a source, it is only a medium. It does not create these potent messages, it only relays them from the creator to you. You and I are human post-offices. We are daily giving out messages of some sort to the world. They do not come from us, but through us; we do not create, we convey. And they come either from hell or from heaven.

Men study how to make their lives more interesting. Take a lesson from the post-office. It is interesting, not because of itself, but because of what it passes on to men. The world will make a beaten path to your door if you bring them news from heaven. What letters go thought the window of your life? Letters of truth and hope, to cheer and console? Or do you hand out dirty trash, worthless drivel, black-edged missives of misery?

Every Christian is a postmaster for God. His duty is to pass out good news from above. If the postmaster kept all the mail and refused to give it out, he would soon be in trouble. No wonder some Christians are so miserable: they keep God's blessings within their own little lives, and soon there is congestion. God does not send us good things from the heavenly headquarters merely for our personal enjoyment. Some of them may be addressed to us, but most of them belong to our fellow-men, and we must pass them on.

He would be a poor postmaster who spent his time decorating the post-office and failed to distribute the mail. For people do not come there to see the post-office: they come for the mail. The Christian seriously misunderstands his work as God's postmaster if he spend his time decorating his place of business and neglect to deliver God's messages through him to men. To be sure, a clean and tidy post-office is desirable, and so is a holy life: but it is easy for one to become so engrossed in introspection that he make his goodness his business. Keeping our lives clean is only tidying up the office to carry on God's business. If it is an end in itself, nothing passes out to men.

How thrilling the plainest life can be when it becomes a function in God's great system and not a selfish enterprise! The tiniest post-office can bear a letter that may wreck or bless a nation. And the simplest life can relay blessings that may rock a continent toward God.

If you are a believer, you are God's postmaster in the little nook where you live. Keep the office clean, but do not make that more important than delivering the messages. Men will soon learn to gather at the window and will bring you, in return, letters of their own to pass on to others.

XXIX

"BACK HOME"

TODAY there came a letter from the folks back home, from the little house in the hills where this poor scribe dreamed the long, long dreams of youth. They tell me that spring has come again: "the woods are green and the mocking-bird is singing." That is enough! They needn't tell me any more! I know the rest, and I'm up and away on the wings of fancy, heading straight back home!

Yonder is the old house among the oaks and the plain dirt road by it. I'm crossing the pasture fence and bound for the hollow. Here is the little old branch running right through the middle of the woods; yonder is the old sawmill place and up there is my pine thicket. I hear the wood-thrush chiming from the big oak down by the spring. It is late afternoon and I climb the hill again just in time to see sundown along the Blue Ridge skyline while the night-hawk "zooms" above and the whippoorwill marks the end of a perfect day.

"The woods are green and the mocking-bird is singing!" How soothing to tired and fevered nerves is a little breath like that from old joys

and simple things back home! We all are getting
pretty well frayed in the mad pandemonium of
these frenzied times. What with making a living
and paying debts and keeping abreast of the times
and up with the Joneses, some of us are sadly ad-
dled and not sure most of the time whether we are
going or coming. It is good to forget it all once in
a while, drop back in our chair, and reflect that the
feverish developments of these frantic times have
not kept spring from coming back home. "The
woods are green and the mocking-bird is singing"
as in other days "when we were so happy an' so
pore."

Thank God, some dear old things do not change.
We work ourselves into a mental and spiritual St.
Vitus. We make mountains out of our molehill
concerns and think wisdom will die with us. It is
refreshing to remember that, long after our stormy
issues have been forgotten, plain things like spring
and mocking-birds will endure. Why so hot, little
man? You are dizzy from modernity's merry-go-
round. Your storming and shouting will bring you
only high blood-pressure. Calm yourself: "the
woods are green and the mocking-bird is singing"
back home!

In the realm of things religious, some of us have
grown weary of so much controversy and debate.
We believe more than ever before in the faith of

our fathers, but we are tired of so many pugna-
cious defenders of it who yell themselves hoarse
over pet notions and extreme interpretations. We
like to reflect that, back of it all, God loves us;
Jesus died for us; and he that believeth shall not
perish, but have everlasting life.

God help us, sorely pressed as we are in these
terrific times, in patience to possess our souls!
Help us to steer between the Scylla of cold indiffer-
ence and the Charybdis of overwrought emotional-
ism! Alas, we are too serious over what we ought
to take lightly, and too lightly do we take what is
most serious! The things upon which we bestow
our time and thought are not worth them, and the
things for which we have no time, things simple
and eternal, are the matters for which, eventually,
we must take time.

Let me relax, throw open the windows of my
stuffy little soul and let the cooling breezes of a
better world sweep through! What will all my
petty worries amount to fifty years from now? I
will rejoice in the old simplicities which no man
can take away—like spring and green woods and
mocking-birds. And, better still, I will rest my
soul in the goodness of God and His amazing grace,
that saves a poor sinner like me.